BOGOTA
TRAVEL GUIDE 2023

The Ultimate Bogota Guide, Everything you need to know, unveiling Hidden Gems & Must See Attractions in Bogota, Colombia

BETTY R COSS

COPYRIGHT

All Rights Reserved.
No part of this publication may be reproduced, distributed, or transmitted in any form or by any means, including photocopying, recording, or other electronic or mechanical methods, without the prior written permission of the owner.

COPYRIGHT © BETTY R CROSS

TABLE OF CONTENTS

COPYRIGHT	1
TABLE OF CONTENTS	3
INTRODUCTION	4
GETTING READY FOR YOUR TRIP	10
GETTING TO BOGOTA	18
ACCOMMODATION OPTIONS	24
NAVIGATING BOGOTA	32
EXPLORING BOGOTA'S CULTURE	39
MUST-SEE ATTRACTIONS	48
HIDDEN GEMS	58
OUTDOOR ADVENTURES	65
SHOPPING IN BOGOTA	72
NIGHTLIFE & ENTERTAINMENT	79
DAY TRIPS FROM BOGOTA	86
SAFETY & PRACTICAL TIPS	95
CONCLUSION	103
APPENDIX	108

INTRODUCTION

I knew my experience had started when I got off the aircraft in Bogota. In the busy airport, I couldn't help but feel eager as the cool mountain air welcomed me like an old friend. Bogota, the capital of Colombia, drew me in with its promises of a thriving culture, breathtaking scenery, and life-changing encounters.

Welcome to Bogota, Colombia

The capital of Colombia, Bogota, is a city of fascinating contrasts and is located at an elevation of 2,640 metres (8,660 feet) above sea level, deep inside the Andes Mountains. Welcome to a city where colonial architecture coexists with modern art, where enduring customs and cutting-edge technology coexist together. The centre of Colombia is located here; it is a city with a fascinating past and a promising future.

Bogota is ready to share its rich culture, delectable cuisine, and breathtaking vistas with visitors and does so with open arms. You'll notice the crisp mountain air as soon as you walk off the aircraft at El Dorado International Airport, serving as a constant reminder of the city's unusual elevation. You will feel at home among the "Rolas" or "Rolos," who are famed for their friendliness and contagious enthusiasm for showing you about their city.

Why Travel to Bogota in 2023?

Here are numerous convincing arguments as to why 2023 is a great year to start your Bogota adventure:

i. Rejuvenated Tourism: To improve accessibility and enjoyment for tourists, Bogota has been aggressively investing in its tourism infrastructure. Your journey will be easy and pleasurable thanks to new hotels, better transit alternatives, and increased safety precautions.

ii. Cultural Renaissance: There has been a rebirth in Bogota's art and culture landscape. Exhibitions, music festivals, and theatrical productions keep the city vibrant. Whether you love art or are just inquisitive, there is a vibrant cultural environment to discover.

iii. *Historical Significance:* Bogota is a city rich in history since it is Colombia's political and cultural centre. Significant historical anniversaries will be celebrated in 2023, providing a special chance to interact with Colombia's history and present. Explore Bogota's museums and historic areas to get a glimpse of the city's rich legacy.

iv. *Natural Beauty:* Beyond its busy streets, Bogota is blessed with breathtaking natural beauty. The city is surrounded by beautiful mountains that provide chances for hiking, riding, and exploring pristine surroundings for adventure lovers. The year 2023 seems to be a great one for ecotourism in Bogota.

v. *Culinary Delights:* Creative chefs are reinventing classic Colombian dishes as the cuisine undergoes a revival. Don't pass up the opportunity to sample regional delicacies and top-notch cuisine in Bogota's diversified eating scene.

vi. *Festivals & Events:* The year 2023 is jam-packed with thrilling events, from the spectacular Bogota Carnival to the Bogota International Film Festival. These events are ideal for experiencing Colombian culture firsthand and making priceless memories.

How to Use This Guide

This in-depth travel guide to Bogota is created to be your invaluable travel companion. Here's how to get around it successfully:

i. *Planning Your Adventure:* Exploring the "Getting Ready for Your Trip" portion of portion 2 should be your first step in planning your adventure. To guarantee a smooth start to your vacation, you'll find below some priceless advice on visa requirements, travel insurance, and packing necessities.

ii. *Exploring Bogota:* Discover the heart of Bogota with our in-depth coverage of the area's neighbourhoods, points of interest, and undiscovered treasures. The information in Sections 4 to 8 covers lodging alternatives, travel, cultural activities, must-see landmarks, and surprises.

iii. *Adventurous Escapes:* Section 9 can help you organise thrilling day excursions to the natural marvels that surround Bogota. The adjacent communities of Villa de Leyva and the Zipaquirá Salt Cathedral may all be reached as well as hiking in the Andes.

iv. *Immerse Yourself in Culture:* Section 6 explores the diverse cultural landscape of Bogota. Explore the city's lively cultural scene, delight in its food, and learn about its history.

v. *Nightlife & Entertainment:* Section 11 has you covered if you want to explore the city after dark. Discover Bogota's vibrant clubs, robust music scene, and vibrant theatre scene.

vi. *Safety & Practical Advice:* Section 13 offers advice on how to keep safe in Bogota, as well as local etiquette, language suggestions, and money management.

With this book in your hands, you're prepared to go across Bogota on a riveting adventure, discovering its secrets and taking in the warmth and charm of Colombia's capital city in 2023. Whatever your interests—history, nature, art, or just being an adventurous traveller—Bogota has something unique in store for you. Welcome to your once-in-a-lifetime journey!

GETTING READY FOR YOUR TRIP

While setting off on a Bogota adventure is thrilling, careful planning is essential for a hassle-free trip. The crucial components of preparing for your trip will be covered in this area, from planning and visa requirements to travel insurance and necessary items to bring.

Planning Your Bogota Adventure

Travellers may choose from a wide variety of experiences in Bogota, the capital of Colombia. Your journey might be more fun and hassle-free if you plan. Here are some crucial things to remember:

i. *Dates of Travel:* Consider your options carefully. Bogota's height causes the weather to change throughout the year. While the wet season, which lasts from April to November, may sometimes bring rain, the dry season, which lasts from December to March, is great for outdoor activities. When choosing a time to visit, take your preferences into account.

ii. *Duration of Stay:* Determine the length of your planned stay in Bogota. Longer visits provide a more thorough investigation of the city and its surroundings. A typical visit might be anything from a few days to a week.

iii. *Budget:* Establishing a budget can help you plan your vacation. Although Colombia is renowned for its affordability, it is essential to make plans for lodging, travel, food, and activities.

iv. *Itinerary:* Make a basic schedule listing the locations and sites you plan to see. By doing this, you can maximise your time in Bogota and make sure you don't miss any must-see attractions.

v. *Health Precautions:* Before flying to Bogota, check with your doctor about any recommended vaccines or health measures. Due to the city's high height, altitude sickness is a problem; as a result, think about acclimatising for a day or two when you first arrive.

Entry Requirements and Visas

To prevent any travel hiccups, it is essential to comprehend Colombia's visa and entrance regulations. What you need to know is as follows:

i. *Tourist Visa:* Many visitors may enter Bogota without a visa for stays up to 90 days. This applies to nationals of a wide range of nations, including the US, Canada, the EU, and the majority of South American nations. The official Colombian government website or the Colombian embassy or consulate in your country should be consulted for the most recent information since admission requirements are subject to change.

ii. *Validity of Passport:* Ensure that your passport is valid for at least six months after the day you want to leave Colombia. Many nations, including Colombia, have this as a standard requirement.

iii. *Entry Stamp:* You'll get an entry stamp on your passport when you arrive. This document, which acts as evidence of your authorised admission into Colombia, should be kept securely.

iv. *Visa Extensions:* This is an option if you want to remain in Colombia beyond the original 90-day period allowed by your visa. But before your first visa expires, you must request an extension. For the most recent information and application processes, contact the Colombian immigration authority

Travel Insurance & Safety Tips

During your vacation in Bogota, it is crucial to ensure your safety and well-being. Here are some suggestions for safety and travel insurance:

i. *Travel Insurance:* Purchase comprehensive travel insurance that includes coverage for medical emergencies, trip cancellations, and lost or stolen possessions. Verify that high-altitude locations like Bogota are expressly covered by your insurance coverage.

ii. *Safety Precautions:* Despite recent safety improvements, it's still important to use common sense safety measures in Bogota. Use trusted transportation, stay in places with good reviews, and avoid flaunting expensive stuff.

iii. *Altitude Sickness:* Due to the area's high elevation, some visitors may develop altitude sickness symptoms. Take it easy for the first day or two, hydrate well, and stay away from big foods and alcohol to let your body adjust.

iv. *Emergency Numbers:* Write down or memorise the local 911 number, the number for the closest embassy or consulate, and the phone number for your travel insurance company.

v. *Local Laws & Customs:* Become familiar with the local laws and customs. Although Colombians are often kind and hospitable, it is important to respect their customs and culture. Due to Colombia's severe anti-drug legislation, be aware of local regulations prohibiting drug possession.

Packing Essentials

For your excursion in Bogota, packing wisely might increase your comfort and enjoyment of the trip. Here is a list of crucial things to think about:

i. *Clothing:* Dress in layers to meet a range of temperatures. For warmer days, wear lighter clothes, while for chilly nights, wear a jacket or sweater. For city exploration, don't forget a pair of suitable walking shoes.

ii. *Rain Gear:* It's a good idea to carry a small umbrella and a waterproof jacket if you're travelling during the rainy season.

iii. *Travel Adapters:* Travel adapters are required since Colombia utilises 110V Type A and Type B outlets. Make sure you have the necessary voltage converters and travel adapters, if applicable.

iv. Medication: Bring any prescription copies you may need, as well as any essential medicines. Bogota has pharmacies, however, it's advisable to carry your important drugs with you.

v. Travel Documents: Store all of your trip papers, such as your passport, visa information, travel insurance policy information, and itinerary, in a safe, water-resistant bag.

vi. Cash and Payment Methods: Although credit cards are generally accepted in Bogota, it is still a good idea to have some local currency on hand for smaller transactions, and in case you visit locations where card acceptance is spotty. To prevent card problems, let your bank know about your vacation intentions.

vii. Health & Hygiene Items: Pack any personal hygiene products you desire as well as any over-the-counter medicines you may need. Don't forget to bring bug repellent and sunscreen.

viii. *Reusable Water Bottle:* It's important to stay hydrated, particularly at altitude. Bring a refillable bottle of water with you to cut down on plastic waste.

You can guarantee a wonderful and stress-free journey to this alluring Colombian city by meticulously organising your Bogota excursion, remaining educated about entrance regulations and safety measures, and packing sensibly. We'll get into the intricacies of navigating Bogota, learning about its culture, seeing its landmarks, and going on thrilling day excursions in the parts that follow. Prepare to immerse yourself in Colombia's thriving centre.

GETTING TO BOGOTA

With its lively cityscapes and rich cultural legacy, Bogota, the capital of Colombia, attracts visitors from all over the globe. Finding the best airfare, getting to El Dorado International Airport, and using the provided airport transportation are the steps to visiting this fascinating city. We'll walk you through the steps in this part to make sure your arrival in Bogota goes well.

Choose the Best Flight

Choosing the appropriate flight is essential for a convenient and enjoyable trip to Bogota. When choosing a flight, keep the following things in mind:

i. *Departure City:* Your trip to Bogota is probably going to start in your hometown. Look for direct flights from major international airports since they might save you time and improve the convenience of your journey. If a direct flight isn't possible, take into account well-timed layovers that provide easy connections.

ii. *Flight Duration:* There are direct flights to Bogota from several significant locations in the Americas and Europe. The length of your flight might vary greatly depending on where you leave from. Prepare yourself for lengthy trips and think about purchasing a premium class for more comfort.

iii. *Travel Dates:* Being flexible with your trip dates can enable you to get better rates. Use ticket comparison websites and aircraft search tools to find the most affordable travel days and hours. Additionally, travelling off-peak season might result in cheaper flight travel.

iv. *Baggage Allowance:* Verify your preferred airline's baggage policy. To avoid paying for extra baggage, make sure your luggage conforms with the weight and dimension limitations.

v. *Layover Considerations:* If your flight has any stops along the way, consider their length and location. Longer layovers could give you time to visit a different location or just unwind in an airport lounge. Shorter layovers, however, may cut down on total travel time.

Arriving at El Dorado International Airport

Colombia's capital city Bogota is accessible mostly via El Dorado International Airport (BOG). It serves both local and foreign aircraft, making it the busiest airport in the nation. What to anticipate when you arrive at El Dorado Airport is as follows:

i. *Immigration & Customs:* After landing, go to immigration to get an entrance stamp on your passport and to produce your passport. Make sure the details on your passport and other travel papers match.

ii. *Currency Exchange:* You may exchange your money for Colombian pesos at the El Dorado Airport's currency exchange desks. Although it is preferable to convert a modest quantity of money for emergency needs, banks and ATMs in the city often provide higher exchange rates.

iii. *Transportation Information:* Keep an eye out for signs and information counters that list the many ways to get to the city's core. There are several ways to get around El Dorado Airport, including taxis, ride-sharing services, and public buses.

Airport Transportation Options

You have a variety of alternatives for getting about Bogota after landing at El Dorado International Airport:

i. *Taxis:* Taking a taxi to your lodging is a quick and secure option. Outside the terminal, you may hail an official airport taxi by using the appropriate kiosk. Make sure the taxi has a metre at all times, and get a free estimate before setting off on the route.

ii. *Ride-Sharing Services:* In Bogota, businesses like Didi and Uber are available as an alternative to regular taxis. You must download each service's app to utilise it, then use your smartphone to make a ride request.

iii. *Public Buses:* The public bus system in Bogota is called TransMilenio. You may take a free shuttle bus from the airport to the closest TransMilenio station, Portal Eldorado, even though it doesn't have a direct connection to the airport. The huge transportation system of the city is accessible from there. Although this choice is affordable, it may not be the most practical if you have a lot of baggage.

iv. *Private Airport Shuttles:* A few Bogota hotels provide private shuttle services to and from the airport. For hassle-free transport, confirm with your lodging that they provide this service and make the necessary arrangements in advance.

v. *Car Rentals:* Car rentals are available at the airport if you want to explore Bogota and the surrounding area. In the arrivals area, there are counters for the major vehicle rental companies.

vi. *Airport Express:* The Bogota Airport Express is a specialised airport shuttle service that links the airport with several locations across the city, including the historic district. It runs regularly and is an easy alternative for tourists.

El Dorado International Airport is easily accessible from the city, and you may choose the means of transportation that best fits your needs in terms of schedule, price, and preferences. To guarantee a seamless transition from the airport to your Bogota experience, keep in mind that transportation choices and services may change over time. As such, it's a good idea to check for changes closer to your departure date.

We'll get into the intricacies of seeing Bogota in the sections that follow, covering everything from lodging choices to navigating the city's dynamic districts and cultural gems.

ACCOMMODATION OPTIONS

Making the appropriate lodging choices in Bogota is essential to having a relaxing and pleasurable stay in this energetic Colombian metropolis. This part will cover how to choose the ideal lodging, popular areas to stay in, cost-effective lodging alternatives, and opulent getaways. Bogota provides a variety of lodging options to meet your needs, whether you're a frugal tourist or looking for an opulent experience.

Finding the Perfect Place to Stay

Several things need to be taken into account while choosing the ideal location to stay in Bogota, such as your travel preferences, spending limit, and budget. You may use the following advice to make an educated choice:

i. *Define Your Budget:* Decide how much money you have to spend on lodging. From cheap hostels to luxurious hotels, Bogota has accommodations to suit every budget. Your options will be more limited and the selection process will be easier if you are aware of your budget.

ii. *Location Matters:* Think about where in the city you want to be. Are you planning to visit the historic centre, take part in cultural activities, or stay close to commercial areas? Select a neighbourhood in Bogota based on your preferences since each one offers unique benefits.

iii. *Amenities & Services:* Consider the services and facilities you want. Do you prefer a hotel with a spa, an on-site restaurant, or both? Are you searching for a location with meeting spaces or a pool? To assist you in choosing the ideal lodging, make a list of your priorities.

iv. *Travel Season:* The season you go to Bogota may have an impact on both availability and cost. It is important to make reservations in advance since busy tourist seasons may result in increased prices and limited availability. On the other hand, travelling off-peak might result in financial savings.

v. *Reviews & Recommendations:* To determine the calibre and reputation of lodgings, read reviews left by previous visitors on travel websites and forums. Recommendations from friends or other tourists who have been to Bogota may be quite useful.

vi. *Book Directly:* Although third-party booking platforms are useful, think about making a direct reservation with the hotel. When you make a direct reservation, certain businesses may offer lower prices or other benefits, and you may more clearly express any special needs.

Popular Neighbourhoods

The neighbourhoods of Bogota provide a variety of settings and experiences. You may choose to stay in one of the following well-liked areas based on your preferences:

i. La Candelaria: A lovely, energetic district in the city's historic centre that is well-known for its colonial architecture, cobblestone lanes, and cultural landmarks. The city's museums, art galleries, and historical landmarks are easily accessible from this hotel.

ii. Chapinero: A younger, more international audience frequents this area. It's renowned for its hip nightlife, stylish eateries, and welcoming environment for LGBTQ+ people. If you want to be in the thick of Bogota's social scene, Chapinero is a fantastic option.

iii. Zona Rosa & Zona G: The luxury eating and retail choices in Zona Rosa and Zona G are well-known. While Zona Rosa is well-known for its nightlife, Zona G is a gourmet mecca. Both neighbourhoods provide a glimpse of Bogota's opulent lifestyle.

iv. Usaquén: Usaquén is a former colonial neighbourhood that has been transformed into a bohemian enclave. It is known for its artisan markets, upscale boutiques, and tranquil atmosphere. For tourists looking for a more sedate stay, it's an excellent option.

v. *Chico:* As a corporate and financial centre, the Chico district is a practical option for business visitors. Additionally, there are high-end hotels and retail malls there.

vi. *Santa Fe:* Santa Fe is a great choice if you're searching for a central location with easy access to cultural activities and shopping. It provides a choice of luxurious and midrange rooms.

Budget-Friendly Options

Budget-conscious tourists may stay in a choice of comfortable and convenient places to stay in Bogota at reasonable prices. Here are some affordable options:

i. *Hostels:* There is a vibrant hostel culture in Bogota that provides private rooms and dorm-style accommodations at reasonable prices. Common places at hostels make it simple to meet other tourists.

ii. *Guesthouses:* For tourists looking for a cosy setting, guesthouses or guest flats are a great option. If you're travelling in a group or with a family, they may be very cost-effective.

iii. *Budget Hotels:* Budget hostels are widely available in Bogota and provide tidy, cosy rooms at reasonable rates. Search for hotels in convenient areas and with positive visitor ratings.

iv. *Airbnb:* Airbnb provides a variety of lodging alternatives, ranging from individual rooms to complete flats or homes. This might be a cost-effective option, particularly for those who want greater freedom or are planning longer stays.

v. *Local Boutique Hotels:* A few neighbourhood boutique hotels have affordable prices and distinctive features. Consider those with positive visitor ratings and see if they are running any special deals or promotions.

Luxury Retreats

There are many opulent getaways and expensive hotels in Bogota if you're looking for a spectacular and indulgent experience. Here are some luxurious choices to take into account:

i. *5-Star Hotels:* Bogota is home to several five-star hotels, including the Four Seasons, JW Marriott, and The Ritz-Carlton, all of which provide lavish lodgings, first-rate cuisine, and first-rate service.

ii. *Boutique Luxury Hotels:* Explore the boutique luxury hotels in Bogota, which often include distinctive design, individualised service, and unusual features. These hotels offer upscale visitors a more individualised and unique experience.

iii. *Spa & Wellness Resorts:* Several opulent hotels in Bogota include spa and wellness centres, which are great for unwinding and reviving while you're there.

iv. *Exclusive Penthouse Suites:* For the height of luxury, think about reserving an exclusive penthouse suite with 360-degree city views and attentive services.

v. *Private Villas & Retreats:* For those wanting the ultimate solitude and isolation, certain upscale homes in Bogota provide private villas or retreats.

Bogota's hotels and housing options provide a broad range of experiences to meet any traveller's interests, regardless of the kind of accommodations you choose. While touring the fascinating Colombian city, you're sure to discover the ideal lodging, from affordable guesthouses to opulent getaways. The practical elements of getting about in Bogota—from getting around the city to experiencing its vibrant culture and learning about its must-see attractions—will be covered in the sections that follow.

NAVIGATING BOGOTA

The next stage is to tour the city when you arrive in Bogota and have settled into your lodging. Making the most of your vacation requires effective city navigation in Bogota. We'll discuss city transportation alternatives, including public transit, renting a vehicle, and insider tips for navigating the Colombian capital in this part.

Transportation in the City

To assist you in navigating the city's many districts and attractions, Bogota provides a selection of transportation alternatives. An overview of the most frequent commuting options is shown below:

i. Taxis: Taxis are a practical means of transportation and are widely accessible in Bogota. Seek for official yellow taxis that have a taximeter and the business's branding on them. Taxis may be requested on the street, via local businesses like Tappsi, or through ride-hailing applications like Uber. To prevent conflicts about fares, make sure the driver starts the metre at the beginning of the trip.

ii. *Buses:* Bogota has a robust public bus system that makes getting around the city inexpensive. With dedicated bus lanes, the TransMilenio system—identified by its red buses—operates more quickly during rush hour. To utilise the system, you'll need a TransMilenio card. Regular city buses also provide thorough coverage throughout Bogota.

iii. *Cycling:* With designated bike lanes and programs like "EnCicla" and "Bike Mi" for bike sharing, Bogota is renowned for its infrastructure that is bike-friendly. Cycling across the city may be a fun and eco-friendly way to view the sights. Wear the proper safety equipment and observe the traffic laws.

iv. *Walking:* Bogota's small-scale districts make exploring by foot a fun and useful activity. Particularly pedestrian-friendly is the La Candelaria historic quarter, where several sights are conveniently close by.

v. *Ride-Sharing Apps:* Uber and Didi are two ride-sharing services that are available in Bogota and provide a convenient and dependable substitute for conventional taxis. These applications allow you to schedule trips and often include fee estimations as well as the option to make payments online.

vi. *Private Transportation Services:* Some hotels and lodgings provide visitors with private drivers or shuttle services, which may be a handy way to see the city while receiving individualised attention.

Using Public Transport
Bogota's public transportation network comprises the TransMilenio fast transit system, city buses, and a network of shared taxis known as "colectivos." Here are some tips on how to utilise public transportation efficiently:

i. *TransMilenio:* The TransMilenio is a well-liked and speedy method of getting about Bogota. A TransMilenio card, which you can buy at TransMilenio stations, is required to use the system. To access the platform, load money into the card and touch it at the turnstile. Maps and directions are available at every station to aid with navigation.

ii. *City Buses:* Standard city buses offer an inexpensive alternative, although they might be slower and more congested than the TransMilenio. Signs marking bus stations identify the routes that stop there. When boarding the bus, you provide the driver cash to pay the fare.

iii. *Colectivos:* Shared taxis that travel along pre-established routes are known as colectivos. They have set fares and are identifiable by their yellow hue. One may be flagged down on the sidewalk or at Colectivo stations. When you tell the driver where you are going, they will let you know whether it is on their route.

iv. *Integrated Transport System:* TransMilenio cards often work with the city's other public transportation systems, allowing users to easily switch between several forms of transportation with a single card.

Tips for Getting Around

Consider these useful suggestions to maximise your time in Bogota and guarantee easy navigation:

i. *Traffic Hours:* Be mindful of Bogota's rush hours, which mainly happen in the mornings and evenings of workdays. Plan your activities appropriately to avoid clogged roads.

ii. *Weather Considerations:* Bogota's weather may be erratic and sometimes bouts of rain will occur. Carry an umbrella or raincoat, particularly from April to November when it rains a lot.

iii. *Cash & Payment:* Carry some Colombian pesos on hand for modest transactions as not all businesses take credit cards. It's a good idea to have change on hand for taxis and transit fares.

iv. *Safety:* Be cautious while utilising public transportation or strolling in congested places. Use trustworthy transportation providers, and keep a watch on your possessions.

v. *Language:* While many residents in Bogota are bilingual in English and Spanish, knowing some basic Spanish phrases would make it easier to communicate, particularly in colectivos and taxis.

vi. *Navigation Apps:* Use navigational tools like Google Maps or Waze to make your way around the city, locate public transportation routes, and see current traffic conditions.

vi. *Altitude Considerations:* Remember that Bogota's high elevation might have an impact on your physical health. Take it easy for the first day or two to let your body adjust, if necessary.

v. *Street Addresses:* Bogota's distinctive "Carrera" and "calle" addressing systems designate the north-south and east-west directions of streets, respectively. This system must be understood to move about the city.

Bogota might be difficult to navigate at first, but with little planning and knowledge of your alternatives, you can get about the city quickly and comfortably. Bogota's many districts and attractions are waiting for you to explore, whether you decide to take a cab, use public transportation, or choose to hire a vehicle. We'll explore the many cultural experiences, must-see sights, and gastronomic treats that make Bogota such an alluring vacation destination in the sections that follow.

EXPLORING BOGOTA'S CULTURE

Bogota is a city with a vivid history in terms of culture. You should delve into the city's history, savour its gastronomic pleasures, take part in its festivals and events, and embrace its vibrant arts and cultural scene if you want to experience this enthralling Colombian capital. We'll go deep into learning about Bogota's culture in this part.

Bogota's History and Heritage

The history of Bogota is weaved together from elements of indigenous civilizations, Spanish colonisation, and a lively fusion of many influences. Investigating the city's historical foundations is crucial to understanding its culture:

i. *Colonial Legacy:* La Candelaria, Bogota's historic district, is a tangible reminder of the city's colonial heritage. Stroll through streets packed with colonial buildings that have been maintained, such as churches, houses, and museums. The magnificent Iglesia of San Francisco and the Casa de la Moneda are two noteworthy locations.

ii. *Museums:* Bogota is home to a wide variety of museums that provide insights into the history and culture of Colombia. The National Museum (Museo Nacional) explores the history of the country via art, archaeology, and anthropology, while the Gold Museum (Museo del Oro) displays a sizable collection of pre-Columbian gold artefacts.

iii. *Era of Independence:* Visit Simon Bolivar's old home, the Quinta de Bolivar, to learn about Colombia's struggle for independence. Bolivar played a crucial role in the liberation of South America from Spanish tyranny. The on-site museum provides a window into the country's battle for independence.

iv. *Indigenous Communities:* Indigenous communities with rich cultural histories surround Bogota, including the Muisca people.

To learn about indigenous customs and history, think about going to surrounding towns like Zipaquira, which is home to the renowned Salt Cathedral (Catedral de Sal).

v. *Colonial Churches:* Bogota is peppered with exquisite churches that highlight the design and craftsmanship of the colonial era. A good example is the 19th-century Catedral Primada de Bogotá, as well as the Santa Clara Church with its magnificent baroque altar.

Local Cuisine and Dining

The delicious taste mix of Colombian food is influenced by indigenous, Spanish, African, and Caribbean influences. The food scene in Bogota offers a window into the city's culture:

i. *Ajiaco:* Ajiaco is a classic Colombian soup that you must sample when visiting Bogota. This filling recipe combines chicken, three different kinds of potatoes, corn, capers, and a little bit of cream to make a delectable and cosy supper.

ii. *Bandeja Paisa:* Although this hearty Colombian dish originates from the Antioquia area, you may get it in Bogota. Beans, rice, ground beef, chorizo, chicharrón (fried pig belly), plantains, avocado, and a fried egg are frequently included.

iii. *Empanadas:* Colombian empanadas are a well-liked snack. These dough pockets are deep-fried and often stuffed with cheese, meat, or chicken. Aji sauce is frequently given on the side for taste.

iv. *Arepas:* There are many different varieties of this essential dish in Colombian cooking. These cornmeal-based, spherical flatbreads may be loaded with cheese, meat, or other ingredients. They are often eaten as a side dish or snack.

v. *Coffee:* Colombia is well-known for its brews, and Bogota is where you can sample some of the finest. To experience the many tastes of Colombian coffee, which vary by area, visit nearby coffee shops.

vi. *Street Food:* Cuisine carts selling great and reasonably priced street cuisine fill the streets of Bogota. Try the almojábanas (cheese bread), chocoramo (a chocolate pastry), and papas rellenas (stuffed potatoes).

vii. *Fruit Markets:* Explore the thriving fruit markets in Bogota, such as Paloquemao Market, to find a variety of unusual fruits and drinks that are only available in Colombia. Try guanabana, maracuya, and lulo fruits, as well as freshly squeezed juices.

viii. *Local Cuisine:* For a Colombian eating experience, look for neighbourhood "fondas" or "corrientazos" eateries. These restaurants often provide corrientazos, daily specials that offer a complete meal at a reasonable price.

Festivals and Events

The annual schedule of festivals and events in Bogota brings the city to life and provides a window into its thriving culture.

i. *Carnival of Bogota (Carnaval de Bogotá):* This festival takes place in August in honour of the city's origin with parades, music, dancing, and vibrant costumes. Experience the fervour and enthusiasm of the city during this festive season.

ii. *Bogota International Film Festival:* This Festival, which usually takes place in October, will be enjoyed by movie buffs. It draws filmmakers and movie lovers from all over the globe with its varied collection of foreign and Colombian films.

iii. *Rock al Parque:* If you like live music, schedule your trip to coincide with one of Latin America's biggest free rock music events, Rock al Parque. It takes place in July and involves both local and foreign rock acts, attracting large audiences to the parks of Bogota.

iv. *Festival Iberoamericano de Teatro de Bogotá:* This famous Festival is held every two years and features a variety of theatrical shows, from traditional plays to avant-garde works. It's a celebration of both foreign and domestic theatre.

v. ***Feria Internacional del Libro de Bogotá (FILBo):*** Book enthusiasts might think about going to Bogota at the annual International Book Fair which is usually held in April. The FILBo offers a wide range of books in many genres, literary activities, and book presentations.

Arts and Culture Scene

The artistic and cultural landscape of Bogota is vibrant, with a wide range of venues and organisations devoted to displaying both national and international talent:

i. ***Museo de Arte Moderno de Bogotá (MAMBO):*** MAMBO is Bogota's top modern art gallery, housing a significant collection of both local and foreign contemporary works. It often holds cultural events, seminars, and exhibits.

ii. ***Biblioteca Luis Angel Arango:*** The Bogota cultural centre, Biblioteca Luis Angel Arango, has a sizable collection of books, music, and artwork. Visit its huge collection and take in any on-site talks, performances, or exhibits.

iii. *Teatro Colon:* The Teatro Colon is a famous performing arts centre and the main opera theatre of Bogota. For information on ballet, opera, classical concerts, and theatrical performances, see the schedule.

iv. *Street Art:* Vibrant street art and murals enliven the streets of Bogota. Explore the city's inventiveness and social criticism via urban art by taking a walking tour around areas like La Candelaria.

v. *Concerts & Live Music:* The music scene in Bogota is diverse, with venues holding live performances in a range of genres, from jazz to rock to electronic music. To find concerts and music festivals, check your local listings.

vi. *Dance:* Attend dance performances including traditional Colombian dances like cumbia, vallenato, and salsa to get a feel for the rhythm of the country. Visitors may take dancing lessons at several places.

vi. *Theater & Performance Art:* The theatres in Bogota provide a variety of productions, including traditional plays as well as experimental theatre and performance art. For future performances, check the calendars of theatres like Teatro Libre and Teatro Nacional.

vii. *Literary Cafés:* Bogota's "cafés ," or literary cafes, provide comfortable spaces for reading, writing, and discussing literature. Poetry evenings and book readings are often held at these cafés.

Through its history, gastronomy, festivals, and cultural scene, Bogota's culture expresses a dynamic blend of its past and present. You will have a greater understanding of Bogota's distinctive personality and the kind hospitality of its people by learning more about these facets of the city's culture. The must-see sights and undiscovered jewels of Bogota that should be on every traveller's itinerary are highlighted in the section after this one.

MUST-SEE ATTRACTIONS

The vivacious city of Bogota, which serves as Colombia's capital, is home to a wealth of must-see sites and tourist attractions. Bogota invites visitors to discover its wide range of attractions, including its world-class museums, gorgeous vistas, lovely colonial neighbourhoods, and even an incredible salt cathedral. We'll walk you through some of the best sights that you should include on your itinerary for Bogota in this section.

La Candelaria: Historic Heart of Bogota

La Candelaria, located in Bogota's historic centre, is a district with colonial buildings, cobblestone lanes, and a strong cultural legacy that takes you back in time. What must you not miss at La Candelaria is as follows:

i. *Plaza de Bolivar:* Start your trip in Plaza de Bolivar, the city's central plaza, which is bordered by famous buildings like the Capitol, the Presidential Palace (Casa de Nario), and the Bogota Cathedral. It is a centre of political and historical importance.

ii. *Iglesia de San Francisco:* Known for its elaborate interior and beautiful altarpieces, this 16th-century church is a remarkable example of Spanish colonial architecture.

iii. *Museo Botero:* A well-known Colombian artist, is the subject of an extraordinary collection of works on display at the Museo Botero, including his recognizable chubby figures and exquisite paintings and sculptures.

iv. *Museo de la Independencia:* The Casa del Florero is home to the Museo de la Independencia, a museum that chronicles Colombia's struggle for independence via historical relics and displays.

v. *Chorro de Quevedo:* This charming plaza is regarded as Bogota's birthplace. It's a popular meeting area for residents, musicians, and artists, and it's a terrific location to listen to live music and eat street cuisine.

vi. *Casa de Moneda:* Visit the Casa de Moneda, a former mint in Colombia that is now a museum where you can study the development of coins and banknotes and learn about the history of money.

vii. *Street Art:* La Candelaria is renowned for its colourful murals and street art. Discover the urban art that covers the city's walls and conveys important social and cultural narratives by taking a walking tour.

viii. *Teatro Colón:* Teatro Colón is a historic theatre that often holds ballet, opera, and musical acts if you're interested in the performing arts.

Gold Museum (Museo del Oro)

One of Bogota's crown jewels is the Gold Museum, or Museo del Oro, which houses a remarkable collection of pre-Columbian gold artefacts. For lovers of history and art, it is a must-see:

i. *Gold Treasures:* The museum has one of the largest collections of its sort in the world, with more than 55,000 pieces of gold. Enjoy exquisite sculptures, jewellery, and other items made for ceremonies by indigenous civilizations.

ii. *Cosmology & Culture:* The displays examine the cosmology and cultural customs of Colombia's indigenous cultures, illuminating the importance of gold in their rites and activities.

iii. *Interactive Displays:* The museum has interesting interactive exhibits that provide light on the design and meaning of the gold objects. It's an immersive learning experience.

iv. *Special Exhibitions:* Check the museum's calendar for any upcoming special exhibits and activities, many of which focus on the history, archaeology, and indigenous cultures of Colombia.

Montserrat Hill

A well-known natural landmark, Monserrate Hill provides sweeping views over Bogota and the area's topography. What to anticipate at this high attraction is as follows:

i. *Funicular or Cable Car:* There are two ways to go up Monserrate Hill: a funicular train or a cable car. Both approaches provide a beautiful ascent of the mountain.

ii. *Viewpoints:* From the peak, gaze out across Bogota's expansive metropolis and the Andes Mountains that surround it. It's a well-liked location for pictures and quiet reflection.

iii. *Basilica of the Fallen Lord:* The ancient Basilica Santuario del Senor Cado de Monserrate is located in Monserrate. People pay their respects to the Fallen Lord and take part in religious rituals when they go to the basilica.

iv. *Hiking:* Some routes lead to the peak for the more intrepid tourist. A different viewpoint is provided by the hike to Monserrate, which is a worthwhile outdoor adventure.

Botero Museum

A cultural treasure of La Candelaria is the Botero Museum, which showcases the creations of renowned Colombian artist Fernando Botero. What makes this museum a must-see is listed below:

i. *Botero's Artistry:* The museum's collection features a wide variety of the artist's paintings and sculptures, showing his distinctive style distinguished by oversized figures and exaggerated dimensions.

ii. *International Art:* The museum's excellent collection of international art includes pieces by well-known artists including Picasso, Dali, and Monet in addition to those by Botero.

iii. *Free Admission:* The greatest thing is that admission is free. All visitors to the Botero Museum are granted free entrance, making it open to both art enthusiasts and inquisitive tourists.

iv. *Cultural Events:* The museum sometimes hosts educational programs, temporary exhibits, and cultural events that enhance the tourist experience.

Usaquén: A Charming Colonial District

Usaquén is a charming colonial neighbourhood in Bogota that provides a pleasant diversion from the busy city centre. What to discover in Usaquén is as follows:

i. *Plaza de Usaquén:* The centre of this picturesque area, Plaza de Usaquén, is where you should begin your journey. Colonial-era houses, artisan stores, and charming cafés along the square's perimeter.

ii. *Sunday Market:* If you go on a Sunday, be sure to check out the Usaquén Flea Market. It's a lively outdoor market where you can buy apparel, street food, antiques, crafts, and antiquities.

iii. *Iglesia de Santa Barbara:* This stunning church, which serves as Usaquén's main attraction, is distinguished by its charming blue and white front. The inside is similarly stunning and includes elaborate altarpieces.

iv. *Culinary Delights:* Usaquén is well-known for its eating establishments. Investigate the area's eateries, which provide a wide variety of food, from traditional Colombian meals to foreign cuisine.

v. *Art Galleries:* Usaquén has several art galleries, giving it a perfect destination to discover regional and modern art. Check out the exhibits at NC-arte and Espacio El Dorado.

Zipaquirá Salt Cathedral Excursión

The Zipaquirá Salt Cathedral is a fascinating adventure that is just a short drive from Bogota, while not being in the city itself. It's a stunning salt mine church that was constructed underground:

i. *Religious Significance:* For Catholics and Colombians, the Salt Cathedral is an important religious location. It has multiple salt rock chambers and chapels with exquisite cross-shaped carvings and religious symbolism.

ii. *Architecture & Art:* The cathedral's design, complete with lit salt sculptures and subterranean plazas, is breathtaking. It combines the wonders of nature, spirituality, and art.

iii. *Light & Sound Show:* Experience the cathedral's spectacular light and sound performance, which heightens the sensory and spiritual trip within the subterranean chambers.

iv. *Cultural Experience:* The trip to Zipaquirá gives both a spiritual and cultural experience. You'll discover the history and economic importance of salt mining in the area.

Practical Tips: Before making travel arrangements, confirm the location's hours of operation and any applicable safety precautions. Getting to the cathedral early is advised since it might become busy.

These Bogota must-sees provide a variety of experiences, from getting lost in history and culture to enjoying Colombian cuisine and seeing magnificent natural settings. Every tourist will find something in Bogota to pique their interest, whether they are interested in history, art, or just the beauty of a place. We'll go into the specifics of your trip to Bogota in the next part, including advice on how to be safe, mingle with the people, and enjoy yourself.

HIDDEN GEMS

Intrepid tourists should visit Bogota to find all of its hidden treasures. While the city's well-known sights are undoubtedly worthwhile seeing, there is also a vast array of lesser-known gems, including specialised museums, bright street art, undiscovered parks, and lively local markets and food stalls. We'll reveal some of Bogota's best-kept secrets in this area.

Lesser-Known Museums

Several museums in Bogota are not on the beaten route. These lesser-known museums provide special perspectives on many facets of Colombian history and culture:

i. *Museo Santa Clara:* The Santa Clara Church is home to the Museo Santa Clara, a modest museum that displays religious artwork and artefacts from the colonial period, including paintings, sculptures, and religious objects.

ii. *Museo de Trajes Regionales:* Discover Colombia's rich textile traditions at this museum, which features a varied array of traditional apparel from throughout the nation.

iii. *Museo del Chico:* This museum, which is tucked away in the Chico district, displays items from Mercedes Sierra de Perez's collection of furniture, artwork, and decorative items from Europe and Colombia.

iv. *Museo Arqueológico:* Discover ancient Colombian history at this museum, which features a variety of pre-Columbian ceramics, sculptures, and jewellery among other objects.

v. *Museo Militar:* The Military Museum has a sizable collection of military relics, equipment, uniforms, and records that shed light on Colombia's military past and appeal to history aficionados.

Exploring Bogota's Street Art

The flourishing street art movement in Bogota is evidence of the city's ingenuity and tenacity. Bogota is full of street art, but several neighbourhoods have particularly good examples:

i. *Calle 26:* Explore Calle 26, a section of road that leads to the airport, where vibrant murals decorate the walls and tell tales of Bogota's recent and recent past.

ii. *San Felipe:* Fans of street art flock to the San Felipe district. Discover spectacular murals and urban art as you stroll the city's streets; these works often express social and political issues.

iii. *La Perseverancia:* This area is well-known for its efforts in urban art. Admire the paintings, graffiti, and installations that represent the city's many cultural influences as you stroll through the streets.

iv. *Hippies Park (Parque de los Hippies):* A popular hangout for creative types, musicians, and other bohemian types in Chapinero. It's a great place to take in the local street art culture as well.

v. *Free Walking Tours:* Take part in a street art tour that is organised by regional artists or groups. These tours provide background information and insights into the importance and meaning of the artworks.

Off-the-Beaten-Path Parks

More than only renowned parks like Simón Bolivar Park are available in Bogota. Find some peace by exploring these secret green spaces:

i. *Parque El Virrey:* The Chapinero neighbourhood's Parque El Virrey is a popular place for locals to exercise, have picnics, and people-watch. It often holds exhibitions of art and cultural activities.

ii. *Parque de Los Novios:* Located in the Chapinero Alto neighbourhood, this park is ideal for a tranquil day or evening since it is surrounded by eateries.

iii. *Parque de Los Periodistas:* The Parque de Los Periodistas is a tranquil retreat amid La Candelaria's busy historic district. It's a tranquil spot to unwind after touring the area.

iv. *Jardín Botánico de Bogotá:* Bogota's botanical park, while not fully off the usual path, provides a tranquil respite from the bustle of the city. View its unique plant collections, orchid gardens, and lush foliage.

v. *Parque de Usme:* A lesser-known park in the southern section of Bogota that is renowned for its scenic splendour, hiking routes, and chances to see local species.

Local Markets and Street Food

A gastronomic experience is just waiting to happen in the markets and street food scene of Bogota. Explore these neighbourhood markets to experience true Colombian flavours:

i. *Paloquemao Market:* Paloquemao is one of Bogota's biggest and most well-known marketplaces. It is a bustling centre for fresh food, exotic fruits, flowers, and street cuisine. Try ajiaco and arepas, two classic Colombian foods.

ii. *Mercado de las Pulgas de San Alejo:* Located in Usaquén, this market comes alive every Sunday with a variety of street food vendors, antique shops, and artisan crafters. It's a fantastic location to locate unusual mementos.

iii. *Corabastos Market:* One of the biggest food marketplaces in Latin America, Corabastos Market is an amazing location to see how the city's food supply chain operates. It's not your normal tourist spot, but it gives you a real sense of how people live.

iv. *La Candelaria Street Food:* Keep an eye out for street food sellers selling Colombian treats like empanadas, obleas (thin sweets), and fresh fruit juices as you stroll through La Candelaria's old streets.

v. *Mercado de Las Pulgas:* This flea market, which is close to the Universidad Nacional, sells a variety of used goods, clothes, and street food. Locals visit it, and it offers a window into Bogota's urban life.

vi. *Plaza de Mercado de Las Cruces:* The Las Cruces neighbourhood's Plaza de Mercado de Las Cruces is a great spot to try regional foods like tamales, changua (a milk and egg soup), and almojábanas (cheese bread).

You'll learn more about Bogota's varied culture, creative expressions, and gastronomic traditions when you discover these hidden jewels. To discover Bogota's genuine core, don't be afraid to wander off the usual route. We'll concentrate on useful advice for maximising your Bogota experience in the next part, covering everything from being safe to engaging with locals to mastering city navigation.

OUTDOOR ADVENTURES

Bogota is well-known for its extensive cultural history and urban attractions, but it also provides outdoor adventurers with a variety of thrilling outings among its breathtaking natural surroundings. Bogota's wonderful outdoors lure visitors looking for exhilarating adventures, from trekking in the Andes to bicycling along Ciclova, visiting the Chingaza National Natural Park to finding waterfalls and hot springs. We'll walk you through some of the best outdoor activities Bogota has to offer in this section.

Hiking in the Andes

Bogota is tucked away in the eastern foothills of the Andes Mountains and provides a wealth of hiking possibilities for those who like the outdoors and the natural world:

Quebrada La Vieja: Within the boundaries of the city, Quebrada La Vieja is a well-liked trekking location. The walk leads through luxuriant woodlands and provides sweeping views of Bogota. Despite being a short trek, it offers a wonderful opportunity for a wilderness getaway.

Cerro de Monserrate: You may trek up Cerro de Monserrate in addition to using a cable car or funicular train to get there. The hike provides a strenuous climb with breathtaking views at the summit.

Laguna de Guatavita: Sometimes referred to as the fabled "El Dorado" lake, is located about two hours drive from Bogota. Hike through the verdant foliage that encircles this beautiful crater lake.

Sumapaz Paramo: Visit the high-altitude moorland known as Sumapaz Paramo, which is close to Bogota. Hiking through this untainted wilderness gives you the chance to see rare plants and animals in a tranquil, unspoiled setting.

Chicaque Natural Park: A network of hiking routes through cloud forests with a variety of birding chances, located just outside of Bogota. There are also options for overnight stays in cottages or treehouses.

Ciclovía: Bogota's Bike Path

A cherished custom known as "ciclova" sees streets in Bogota converted into bike lanes and public places for enjoyment on Sundays and public holidays:

i. *Cycling:* Join the residents on the city's streets during Ciclova by renting a bike or bringing your own. You may go at your speed while exploring different neighbourhoods, parks, and monuments. The Usaquén route is a beautiful alternative.

ii. *Rollerblading & Skating:* In addition to cyclists, rollerbladers, and skaters are accepted in Ciclova. It's a great opportunity to take advantage of Bogota's wonderful weather and explore the city from a different angle.

iii. *Street Performers:* There are typically street performers, singers, and vendors offering food and drinks along the Ciclova routes, which contributes to the celebratory mood.

iv. *Exercise Stations:* Some routes on the Ciclova offer exercise stations with exercise gear where you can join residents for a free outdoor workout.

Parque Nacional Natural Chingaza

Parque Nacional Natural Chingaza, a protected national park close to Bogota, is renowned for its pure paramo habitat and hiking trails:

i. *Paramo Hiking:* Hike through the paramo, a rare high-altitude Andean environment in this area. Discover stunning sceneries, including lakes, marshes, and fragile ones (distinctive plants), while hiking along well-marked pathways.

ii. *Birdwatching:* With over 200 different bird species, including the Andean condor and hummingbirds, Chingaza is a birdwatcher's paradise. Bring your binoculars if you want to see these amazing animals.

iii. *Photographing:* Capture the breathtaking panorama of the park, including its misty cloud forests and beautiful lakes.

Excellent picture chances are provided by the day's shifting weather conditions.

iv. *Visitor Centers:* Find out more at the visitor centres about the park's wildlife, plants, and conservation initiatives. For your visit, park rangers may provide you with advice and information.

Waterfalls and Hot Springs

Waterfalls and hot springs are among the many natural attractions in the area around Bogota. These relaxing getaways are excellent for day trips:

i. *La Chorrera Waterfall* is Colombia's highest waterfall, tumbling from a height of almost 590 metres (1,940 feet), and is just a short drive from Bogota. To go to the waterfall and have a cool dip, hike through verdant woodlands.

ii. *Tequendama Falls:* Visit the Tequendama Falls and the old Tequendama Hotel that looks out over the falls. The region is renowned for its picturesque vistas and rich greenery.

iii. *Santa Rosa de Cabal Hot Springs:* Although Santa Rosa de Cabal Hot Springs is a little farther away from Bogota, the trip is worthwhile. Encircled by beautiful foliage, soak in the thermal waters for relaxation and quiet.

iv. *Termas de Juancho:* Termas de Juancho is a tranquil hot spring swimming location near Choach. The mineral composition of the water is thought to offer medicinal advantages.

v. *Hot Springs in Suesca:* A short drive from Bogota, the town of Suesca is home to several hot spring resorts where you can unwind and take advantage of the relaxing effects of thermal waters.

Safety & Environmental Considerations: When doing outdoor activities in the vicinity of Bogota, safety should always come first. Respect park rules, remain on authorised pathways, and heed park ranger instructions. Keep all traces of your actions to a minimum and save the environment for future generations.

Outdoor activities give a chance to engage with nature, take part in physical exercise, and discover the many landscapes that Colombia has to offer.

These activities may be found in and around Bogota. You will have a wonderful experience in Bogota, whether it be trekking in the Andes, cycling along Ciclova, or finding secret hot springs and waterfalls. We'll go into detail about useful advice in the part after this to make sure you have a safe and happy vacation in this energetic Colombian metropolis.

SHOPPING IN BOGOTA

From crowded markets and lively street sellers to upmarket shops and opulent malls, Bogota provides a variety of shopping experiences. This section will lead you through the city's retail district whether you're looking for one-of-a-kind gifts, handmade items, or high-end clothing.

Bogota's Best Shopping Districts

Bogota has several distinctive retail areas, each with its personality and selections:

i. *Zona T (Zona Rosa):* Situated in the Chapinero district, Zona T is renowned for its high-end shops, multinational brands, and exclusive shopping centres like Andino and El Retiro. The area comes alive at night with a large number of pubs and restaurants.

ii. *Usaquén:* The Sunday flea market in Usaquén is a veritable gold mine of handcrafted products, antiques, and artisanal crafts. The neighbourhood's streets are packed with boutique stores that sell one-of-a-kind items of jewellery, apparel, and gifts.

iii. *La Candelaria:* The ancient district of Bogota is filled with stores offering handicrafts, textiles, and other typical Colombian items. Look around Calle 11 and Carrera 6 for genuine trinkets.

iv. *San Victorino* is a thriving commercial area with street vendors, tiny stores, and booths offering a range of things, from apparel and electronics to fresh vegetables, that are ideal for anyone looking for a good deal.

v. *Andean Market:* This market, which is close to Monserrate, focuses on native and Andean crafts. Local craftsmen produce the vibrant fabrics, ceramics, jewellery, and musical instruments you may discover there.

Unique Souvenirs & Handcrafts

Unique trinkets and homemade products are abundant in Bogota and make for treasured keepsakes:

i. *Mochilas:* Indigenous populations in Colombia produce these traditional woven purses. These colourful and detailed bags come in a variety of shapes and designs, making them ideal for carrying daily essentials or used as fashionable accessories.

ii. *Emeralds:* Bogota is a great spot to shop for these priceless jewels. Colombia is known for its emeralds. Find trustworthy jewellers that sell certified emeralds and distinctive jewellery designs.

iii. *Aguayos:* Indigenous people weave these vibrant fabrics, which are used for anything from clothes to ornamental items. They create striking table runners or wall hangings.

iv. *Chocolate:* The taste and quality of Colombian chocolate are well-known. To indulge in a sweet treat or buy presents for loved ones, look for artisanal chocolate stores in Bogota like Cacao Hunters or Cao Artisanal Chocolate.

v. *Coffee:* Colombia is well-known for its coffee, and Bogota has a broad selection of high-end brands and mixes. As a memento, choose freshly roasted beans or ground coffee.

vi. *Chivas:* These vivid, hand-painted buses are scaled-down versions of the brilliant rural buses prevalent in rural areas of Colombia. They make interesting and beautiful keepsakes.

vii. *Sombreros Vueltiaos:* Made from caa flecha palm leaves, sombreros vueltiaos are beautifully woven hats that are native to Colombia's Caribbean area. They are both practical and fashionable.

viii. *Musical Instruments:* Colombian music is varied, and you may buy drums, flutes, and maracas, among other traditional instruments, as mementos. In La Candelaria, look for handcrafted instrument manufacturers.

Luxury Shopping

There are many high-end shopping options in Bogota if you're looking for designer brands and luxury goods:

i. *Andino Mall:* One of Bogota's most prestigious luxury shopping centres, Andino Mall, has upscale clothing, fine jewellery, and worldwide designer retailers. It's a well-liked location for high-end shopping.

ii. *El Retiro Shopping Center:* Next to Andino, El Retiro provides a comparable high-end shopping experience with a variety of known luxury brands and high-end eating establishments.

iii. *Zona T Boutiques:* You may purchase designer apparel, accessories, and luxury products at the posh stores that line the streets around Zona T.

iv. *Designer Showrooms:* In Bogota, a few designers from Colombia sell one-of-a-kind items and apparel that are produced to order. Look for regional designers like Silvia Tcherassi or Esteban Cortázar.

v. *Jewellery Shops:* Emeralds are a popular gemstone in exquisite jewellery made in

Bogota. For excellent items, go to famous jewellers like Caratell or Emerald Center.

Shopping Tips

i. *Negotiation*: Bargaining is widespread at little stores and marketplaces on the streets. Price haggling is encouraged, but remember to be kind and smile while doing it.

ii. *Currency Exchange*: When shopping, particularly at local markets and with street sellers, make sure you have Colombian pesos on hand since they may not take foreign currencies or credit cards.

iii. *Tax Refunds*: If you make certain purchases while travelling, you can be entitled to a VAT refund. Keep your receipts and ask participating retailers how the tax refund procedure works.

iv. *Artisan Markets*: Local artisan markets and fairs, like the handicrafts sector of Paloquemao or Usaquén's Sunday market, provide the greatest assortment of artisanal and handmade items.

v. *Quality Assurance:* To guarantee the authenticity and calibre of your purchase, buy from reputed and licensed merchants when buying things like emeralds or jewellery.

From high-end shoppers and fashion devotees to those looking for one-of-a-kind souvenirs and handmade treasures, Bogota's retail scene has something for everyone. The shopping opportunities in Bogota are as varied as the city itself, whether you like to peruse posh malls, haggle with regional craftspeople, or explore bustling marketplaces.

NIGHTLIFE & ENTERTAINMENT

Bogota evolves into a bustling metropolis with an abundance of nightlife and entertainment choices as the sun sets over the Andes. Bogota has a wide range of nightlife options for residents and tourists alike, including vibrant nightclubs, hip pubs, live music venues, and theatres.

Bogota's Nightclubs and Bars

The nightlife in Bogota is renowned for its variety and ability to accommodate all tastes and preferences. Here are a few of the city's most well-liked pubs and nightclubs:

i. *Theatron:* One of the biggest homosexual clubs in Latin America is called Theatron, and it is situated in the Chapinero neighbourhood. It has many levels, different music genres, themed areas, and a buzzing environment.

ii. *Andrés Carne de Res:* This iconic restaurant and nightclub in Chá, just outside of Bogota, provides a distinctive experience. It has a popular dance floor, live music, and an unusual design.

iii. *Armando Records:* A prominent nightclub in Zona T that attracts both residents and visitors with its blend of live and electronic music. Views of the city are breathtaking from the rooftop patio.

iv. *El Coq:* El Coq is a trendy club and pub with a lively ambiance that is located in the Usaquén area. It's a great location for mingling and enjoying beverages.

v. *Vintrash:* Vintrash is a well-known bar and nightclub in Chapinero Alto. It has a variety of musical genres, including hip-hop, electronic, and reggaeton, and has a young, upbeat feel.

vi. *Casa Jaguar:* Casa Jaguar in Chapinero provides handmade drinks and a nice environment for a more relaxed mood. With friends, it's a fantastic location to relax.

Live Music Venues

If you like live music, Bogota has a strong scene with venues that feature both national and international acts:

i. *Teatro Jorge Eliécer Gaitán:* The historic Teatro Jorge Eliécer Gaitán, located in the city's centre, presents a variety of live acts, such as concerts by well-known performers, plays, and classical music.

ii. *Teatro Colón:* In addition to hosting opera and ballet performances, Teatro Colón sometimes offers live music concerts, providing a distinctive atmosphere for taking in musical productions.

iii. *Cine Tonalá:* This cultural hub in the Chapinero district hosts live music performances, movie screenings, and visual arts displays. It is a creative setting where upcoming regional talent is shown.

iv. *Matik-Matik:* This alternative cultural centre, which is situated in the San Felipe area, often offers avant-garde events, avant-garde art exhibits, and experimental music performances.

v. *Bogota Beer Company (BBC):* Live music evenings featuring regional musicians and artists are held at a few of the company's sites. It's a great way to take in live music and artisan beer.

vi. *Rock Clubs:* With places like Latino Power and El Caracol, Bogota has a flourishing rock music scene. These venues are well-liked by rock fans since they often showcase both regional and worldwide rock musicians.

Theater & Performing Arts

The theatre and performing arts scene in Bogota is vibrant and diversified, providing a range of performances and cultural encounters:

i. *Teatro Nacional La Castellana:* This venue presents a variety of acts, including stand-up comedy, musicals, dramas, and dance performances. View their calendar to learn about future events.

ii. *Teatro Libre:* Teatro Libre is renowned for producing cutting-edge, thought-provoking plays. It often presents modern plays and provides a venue for upcoming performers and authors.

iii. *Teatro Santa Fe:* Located in the Teusaquillo district, Teatro Santa Fe is a distinctive venue for individuals interested in cutting-edge performances. It specialises in experimental and avant-garde theatre.

iv. *Ballet and Dance:* Bogota often hosts ballet and dance performances. Dance groups in the city often present performances of both classical and modern dance.

v. *Cinemas:* Bogota is home to several theatres showing both domestic and foreign films. Throughout the year, other film festivals present both popular and indie movies.

vi. *Cultural Centers:* Theater performances, art exhibits, and literary readings are often held at cultural facilities including Centro Cultural

Gabriel Garca Márquez and Centro Cultural La Media Torta.

Additional Advice

a. *Safety:* It's crucial to use caution and awareness of your surroundings when taking in Bogota's nightlife, particularly in busy locations. Use reliable transportation to go back to your lodging, and keep a watch on your possessions.

b. *Dress Code:* It's a good idea to check ahead of time and wear proper clothing since certain upmarket clubs and events may have dress rules.

c. *Local Events:* To learn about unique events, festivals, and themed parties occurring while you're there, keep an eye on local event listings and social media.

d. *Transportation:* If you're unfamiliar with the city's public transit system, you may want to use ride-sharing apps or pre-arranged transportation to travel to and from nightlife destinations.

Visitors will find something to fit their interests thanks to the many nightlife and entertainment options in Bogota. Bogota provides a dynamic and exciting nightlife experience, whether you're dancing the night away in a buzzing nightclub, taking in live music in a small location, or immersing yourself in the city's theatre and performing arts.

DAY TRIPS FROM BOGOTA

While Bogota has a lot to offer in terms of sights and activities, the area around it is fascinating, with day trip locations that highlight Colombia's natural beauty, cultural legacy, and culinary delights. We'll look at some of the most worthwhile day excursions from Bogota in this section.

Zipaquirá Salt Cathedral
- ***Distance from Bogota:*** Approximately 48 kilometres (30 miles)
- ***Travel Time:*** Approximately 1 hour

Why Visit Zipaquirá Salt Cathedral?
In the depths of the salt mines that run under the town of Zipaquirá, there lies a magnificent technical and spiritual achievement known as the Zipaquirá Salt Cathedral. This underground masterpiece is a tribute to the resourcefulness and religious fervour of Colombians.

What to anticipate

a. *Underground Sanctuary:* Explore the beautiful Salt Cathedral by entering the interior of a mountain. With its lit salt sculptures and crosses, this stunning subterranean area doubles as a tourist destination and a place of devotion.

b. *Religious Significance:* The cathedral has 14 chapels, each of which represents a Station of the Cross, as well as a central nave. For many Colombians and foreigners seeking time for spiritual meditation, it is a notable pilgrimage place.

c. *Light and Sound Spectacle:* To enhance the atmosphere and spiritual experience in the subterranean rooms, the cathedral presents a spellbinding light and sound spectacle.

d. *Cultural Experience:* Beyond the cathedral, Zipaquirá provides options for exploring the town, sampling regional food, and finding traditional handicrafts. The area is also rich in cultural heritage.

e. *Practical Advice:* Before making travel arrangements, confirm the location's hours of operation and any applicable safety precautions. Getting to the cathedral early is advised since it might become busy.

Villa de Leyva: A Colonial Gem
- **Distance from Bogota:** Approximately 160 kilometres (100 miles)
- Travel Time: Approximately 3 hours

Why Visit Villa de Leyva?
With its cobblestone lanes, whitewashed homes, and quaint ambiance, Villa de Leyva is a well-preserved colonial village that takes you back in time. Both history aficionados and those looking for tranquillity should visit.

What to Anticipate
a. *Historic Plaza Mayor:* The Plaza Mayor in Villa de Leyva is one of the biggest town squares in all of South America. It's the perfect area to roam and take in the ambiance since it is surrounded by structures from the colonial period, eateries, and artisan stores.

b. *Fossil Museum (Museo El Fósil):* Visit the Fossil Museum to witness the skeleton of an extinct marine reptile called a kronosaurus as well as other fossilised items discovered in the area.

c. *Religious Architecture:* Visit the Church of Nuestra Senora del Rosario, a stunning example of colonial ecclesiastical architecture. Another historical and architectural treasure is the Convento del Santo Ecce Homo.

d. *Hiking & Outdoor Adventures:* There are hiking and outdoor adventure options in the nearby region. Iguaque Lake and beautiful trails may be found in the neighbouring Iguaque National Park.

e. *Crafts & Souvenirs:* Browse the town's artisan markets and stores for handmade ceramics, clothing, and jewellery.

Coffee Farms Tour
- **Distance from Bogota:** Approximately 120 kilometres (75 miles)
- Travel Time: Approximately 2.5 hours

Why Visit Coffee Farms near Bogota?
Since Colombia is known for its superior coffee, visiting a coffee plantation for the day gives you the chance to learn about the industry and take in the picturesque countryside.

What to Anticipate
a. *Coffee Farm Tours:* Visit coffee farms and learn about the production of coffee from bean to cup on a coffee farm tour. You will be accompanied by knowledgeable guides through the planting, harvesting, and roasting processes.

b. *Coffee Tasting:* During guided tastings of coffee, savour the complex tastes and fragrances of Colombian coffee. You'll learn about the subtle differences between various coffee kinds and brewing techniques.

c. *Scenic Views:* Numerous coffee estates are located in scenic locations, providing breath-taking vistas of gently sloping hills and lush surroundings.

d. *Cultural Insights:* Interact with local producers to learn more about the place of coffee in Colombian culture. Additionally, you'll discover how to produce coffee ethically and sustainably.

e. *Hands-On Experience:* A few coffee farm excursions provide opportunities for visitors to get their hands dirty by selecting their coffee beans or helping to roast them.

Guatavita Lake

- **Distance from Bogota:** Approximately 55 kilometres (34 miles)
- **Travel Time:** Approximately 1.5 hours

Why Visit Guatavita Lake?
Guatavita Lake has a rich history and folklore. It is said that this is where the Muisca people's El Dorado rite, in which gold gifts were thrown into the lake, took place. It is now a picturesque location surrounded by stunning scenery.

What to Anticipate
a. *Scenic Beauty:* The lake is tucked away among verdant hills and woodlands, providing

a serene and lovely backdrop. You may take strolls along the shoreline or go on a trek in the neighbourhood.

b. *Muisca Culture:* Recognize the Muisca culture and the El Dorado mythology, which are closely related to the lake. visit learn more before your journey, head visit the Museo del Oro in Bogota.

c. *Boat Rides:* To enjoy the lake's splendour, take a boat ride on it. Beautiful picture chances result from the nearby hills' reflections in the calm waters.

d. *Cultural and Artisanal Experiences:* Explore the surrounding town of Guatavita, which is renowned for its handicrafts, traditional ceramics, and regional food, for cultural and artistic experiences. It's a lovely location to learn about Colombian culture.

e. *Natural Reserves:* The Guatavita area is also home to natural reserves, such as the Siecha Lakes, where you may go on further hikes and birdwatch.

Tips for Day Trips from Bogota

a. *Transportation:* For day travels from Bogota, think about renting a vehicle, hiring a private driver, or scheduling a guided tour. For these trips, public transportation choices may not be as practical.

b. *Weather:* Be ready for a variety of weather scenarios, particularly if you want to go to remote or high-altitude locations. Layer your clothing and pack drinks and sunscreen, among other necessities.

c. *Local Cuisine:* Take advantage of the chance to try out local fare while on your day outings. Taste the tastes of Colombia's many culinary traditions by trying local delicacies.

d. *Language:* Although many locals in these places may speak Spanish, it's a good idea to know some basic Spanish words and phrases or to utilise translation apps to make conversation easier.

e. *Timing:* To make the most of your time, properly plan your day travels. Consider the travel time to and from Bogota since certain attractions may have set hours for operation.

Day tours from Bogota provide an opportunity to see Colombia's rich cultural legacy, stunning natural surroundings, and distinctive experiences. Each trip deepens and diversifies your Bogota experience, whether you're admiring the Zipaquirá Salt Cathedral, wandering the historic alleyways of Villa de Leyva, enjoying Colombian coffee on a plantation, or thinking about the stories of Guatavita Lake.

SAFETY & PRACTICAL TIPS

A successful and pleasurable trip to Bogota depends on you being safe and knowing the norms and etiquette of the city. We'll provide you with useful advice in this part on how to be safe, respect local customs, use the local language, and take care of your funds while you're there.

Staying Safe in Bogota

Bogota is a lively and friendly city, however, just like any other large metropolis, it's crucial to take safety measures:

i. *Be Aware Of Your Surroundings:* There are many different areas in Bogota, each with its own personality and safety concerns. When planning your trips, do your research and choose well-known, respectable neighbourhoods to stay in, particularly if you're new to the region.

ii. *Street Smarts:* Exercise caution while wandering the streets of the city. Keep your possessions safe and don't flaunt pricey jewellery or high-tech equipment. In crowded places, pickpocketing may happen.

iii. *Use Reputable Transportation:* Choose authorised taxis from reputable businesses, or use ride-sharing services like Didi or Uber. Public transit is typically secure yet congested during peak hours, such as the TransMilenio bus system.

iv. *Cash & ATMs:* Instead of using freestanding machines on the street, use ATMs inside banks or other safe sites. When taking out tiny quantities of money in public, use discretion.

v. *Language Barrier:* Although many people in Bogota know a little English, learning some fundamental Spanish phrases may help you communicate. A phrasebook or translation software may be really helpful.

vi. *Avoid Late-Night Solo Walks:* In general, it's advisable to steer clear of going for a late-night solo stroll, particularly in less-trafficked regions. Use safe transportation choices instead.

vii. *Emergency Numbers:* Call the local police (123) and the emergency medical services (125) if you need to in an emergency. Knowing who to contact in case of an emergency might be quite important.

Local Etiquette & Customs

You may better understand the culture and people of Bogota by adhering to local traditions and etiquette:

i. *Greeting:* A cordial handshake, eye contact, and a warm grin are the typical greetings in Colombia. Unless specifically requested, use titles like "Mr." or "Mrs." before someone's last name when addressing them.

ii. *Politeness:* Colombians place a high priority on decency and respect. In your encounters, generously sprinkle "gracias" (thank you) and "por favor" (please) throughout.

iii. *Personal Space:* Keep your distance from natives while speaking or engaging with them. It is customary for Colombians to stand closer together during chats than you may be used to.

iv. *Dining Etiquette:* It is usual to bring a little gift, like wine or chocolates, to your host's house if you have been invited. It's polite to wait for the host to begin the meal and to finish everything on your plate while you're out to eat.

v. *Tipping:* Tipping is typically accepted at restaurants and while receiving services like cab rides. It is typical to tip between 10% and 15%, but make sure there isn't already a service fee on the invoice.

vi. *Respecting Personal Belongings:* Don't handle or touch another person's items without their consent. This includes accessories and baggage.

v. *Photography:* When photographing individuals, particularly in rural or indigenous cultures, always get their consent. Some people could object to being photographed.

vi. *Respect for Indigenous Cultures:* Find out about the traditions and laws of any indigenous communities you want to visit. There can be limitations on photography and other activities in certain localities.

Language & Communication

Although Spanish is Colombia's official language, the following linguistic considerations might help you communicate in Bogota:

i. *Learn the Basics:* Although many people in Bogotá can speak a little English, it is appreciated when tourists make an effort to do so. Gaining some fundamental language skills may improve your relationships and experiences.

ii. *Translation Apps:* Use your smartphone or download translation applications to quickly translate words as necessary. Popular options include Google Translate.

iii. *Diverse Accents:* Colombia has a wide variety of regional accents and dialects. The accent in Bogota is regarded as neutral and is often simpler to comprehend for outsiders than other regional accents.

iv. *Non-Verbal Communication:* Pay attention to non-verbal indicators, such as gestures and body language, which may improve your ability to comprehend and communicate.

v. *Smile and Patience:* A cheerful smile and persistence go a long way toward overcoming linguistic obstacles. Locals often want to assist and value your attempt at communication.

Money Matters

Effective money management is crucial throughout your visit to Bogota:

i. *Currency:* The Colombian peso (COP) is the nation of Colombia's official currency. To get local money, utilise official exchange services or ATMs and familiarise yourself with the current exchange rate.

ii. *ATMs:* There are several ATMs in Bogota, including those in well-known banks and at malls. Use these to withdraw cash, but be careful of any costs that may apply.

iii. *Credit Cards:* At Bogota, particularly at hotels, eateries, and bigger retailers, major credit cards like Visa and Mastercard are commonly accepted. Carrying some cash is advised for smaller businesses and street sellers, however.

iv. *Bargaining:* Bargaining is widespread among street sellers and at marketplaces. While haggling over costs is okay, be sure you do it courteously and kindly.

v. *Safety Measures:* Carry just the amount of cash you'll need during the day and put additional cash, passports, and other critical papers in a hotel safe. When handling money in public, use discretion.

vi. *Currency Exchange:* To convert currencies, use banks or authorised currency exchange businesses. Beware of unauthorised or unlicensed currency exchangers.

vii. *Keep Records:* Maintain records of your spending, particularly if you intend to apply for a VAT refund for qualifying purchases after you leave the country.

viii. *Check Bills:* Before leaving a restaurant or store, check your bill twice to make sure everything is correct, including any service fees.

You'll be well-equipped to enjoy your vacation to Bogota if you practise good travel hygiene, observe regional traditions, be respectful of others, and handle your money sensibly. These useful suggestions make sure that you can take advantage of all that this dynamic Colombian city has to offer while being secure and experiencing new cultures.

CONCLUSION

It's time to take stock of the amazing trip you've taken and the wide range of experiences you've had in Colombia's capital city as you reach the last pages of our thorough Bogota travel guide. With its thriving arts scene, ancient sites, rich culture, and natural beauties, Bogota has left an everlasting impact on your travel repertory.

Unveiling the Heart of Bogota
We've gone into the heart of Bogota throughout this book, exposing its interesting history, vibrant arts and culture, and stunning scenery. You've become familiar with the city's many areas and their attractions, from the ancient La Candelaria district to the busy Usaquén neighbourhood.

Journey Through Culture
You were exposed to the rich legacy of the city throughout our tour through Bogota's culture. You've strolled around La Candelaria's cobblestone streets, seen works of art at the

Gold and Botero Museums, and savoured regional food. You've participated in lively festivals and danced to the beat of regional music, giving you a thorough understanding of the cultural mosaic that makes up Bogota.

Exploration Beyond the City Limits
You might see the area's historical treasures and natural attractions on day excursions from Bogota. You have seen the variety that surrounds the Colombian capital, from the majestic Zipaquirá Salt Cathedral to the colonial allure of Villa de Leyva. Your Bogota vacation gained depth with these excursions, which also highlighted the nation's varied beauties.

Outdoor Adventures & Hidden Gems
Opportunities for hiking, riding, and fully immersing oneself in Colombia's natural surroundings were made available by the section on outdoor experiences. Undiscovered treasures like obscure museums, street art, parks, and neighbourhood markets gave visitors a look at the real Bogota that is often overlooked by visitors.

Culinary & Shopping Delights
You were exposed to the mouthwatering tastes of Colombian cuisine during your gastronomic exploration of Bogota, from substantial arepas to fragrant ajiaco. The vibrant culinary scene in the city delighted your palate and gave you a better grasp of Colombian cuisine. Additionally, you perused retail areas and looked for one-of-a-kind mementos to bring home from Bogota.

Vibrant Nightlife & Entertainment
The vibrant nightlife of Bogota, as described in Section 11, provided a look inside the city. You've had the chance to enjoy the city's diverse nightlife and entertainment choices, which range from nightclubs and pubs to live music venues and theatres.

Practical Tips & Language Skills
The detailed practical advice offered in Section 13 made sure that you travelled safely, observed local traditions, successfully communicated, and prudently handled your funds while you were there. Your trip was made easy and delightful thanks to these insights.

Remember the friendliness of its people, the depth of its culture, and the breathtaking scenery that has won your heart as you get ready to say goodbye to Bogota. The past and present of Bogota smoothly blend, and every street corner has a tale to tell.

The tapestry of your travel adventures has been woven together by every moment of your Bogota vacation, from taking in the breathtaking vistas from Monserrate Hill to sipping Colombian coffee on a farm. You will always remember the joy you had while mingling with the people, the fragrances of street food filling the air, and the striking colours of the street art.

You are now leaving Bogota, but you are also taking a piece of it with you wherever your adventures may take you. Your life will be further enriched by the knowledge gained and the memories made, which is proof of the value of travel and cultural immersion.

You went on a voyage of discovery in Bogota rather than just visiting a city, and the experiences you had there will always be with you. The lessons you gain here will influence your future journeys, and Bogota will always be a part of your tale.

Consider the knowledge acquired, the relationships formed, and the transformational potential of travel before you go. May you take the spirit of Bogota with you and continue to explore, learn, and appreciate the beauty of our varied planet, regardless of whether your next stop is inside Colombia, on another continent, or closer to home.

We appreciate you picking Bogota as your last stop, and we wish you wonder, curiosity, and the unwavering conviction that every trip is a chance to experience the amazing on your next adventures. Till we meet again, have safe travels!

APPENDICES

You will discover an excellent tool to improve your experience and broaden your knowledge about Bogota and Colombian culture in this last part of the Bogota Travel Guide.

Useful Phrases in Spanish

Although many people in Bogota can speak a little English, making an effort to speak Spanish will help you get about the city and interact with locals. The following words and phrases may improve your communication:

- Hello: **Hola**
- Good morning: **Buenos días**
- Good afternoon: **Buenas tardes**
- Good evening/night: **Buenas noches**
- Yes: **Sí**
- No: **No**
- Please: **Por favor**
- Thank you: **Gracias**
- You're welcome: **De nada**

- Excuse me / I'm sorry: **Perdón / Lo siento**
- Do you speak English?: **¿Hablas inglés?**
- I don't understand: **No entiendo**
- How much does this cost?: **¿Cuánto cuesta esto?**
- Where is...?: **¿Dónde está...?**
- Help: **Ayuda**
- I need a doctor: **Necesito un médico**
- Water: **Agua**
- Food: **Comida**
- Restroom: **Baño**
- Emergency: **Emergencia**
- I'm lost: **Estoy perdido/a**
- Can you recommend a restaurant?: **¿Puede recomendarme un restaurante?**
- What's your name?: **¿Cómo te llamas?**
- My name is...: **Mi nombre es...**
- I'm a tourist: **Soy turista**
- I'd like to buy this: **Me gustaría comprar esto**
- How do I get to...?: **¿Cómo llego a...?**

Even with rudimentary Spanish, using these expressions will be immensely appreciated by the locals and may improve the quality of your conversations.

Printed in Great Britain
by Amazon